MINDFUL CHESS

PAUL VAN DER STERREN

MINDFUL CHESS

*The Spiritual Journey
of a Professional Chess Player*

New In Chess

2024

Contents

Preface

To begin with, let me introduce myself. My name is Paul van der Sterren. I was born in 1956. I'm a Dutch citizen, and I live near Amsterdam in Holland. Throughout most of my adult life I have been a devoted and professional chess player. I won the Dutch Championship twice (in 1985 and 1993), became a Grandmaster in 1989 and represented my country in eight Olympiads from Lucerne 1982 until Istanbul 2000. My best year was 1993, when I won the Zonal Tournament in Brussels, then came second in the Interzonal in Biel and by so doing qualified for the Candidates Matches, the final stage of the then three-yearly cycle to select a challenger for the World Champion. There I lost my first-round match to GM Gata Kamsky in Wijk aan Zee 1994 2½-4½.

I have also been a prolific writer on chess.

During my active years I confined myself mostly to game analyses and short articles for chess magazines. When I quit playing in 2001, larger projects became possible and I wrote a number of books, the most successful of which has been *Fundamental Chess Openings* (published by Gambit in 2009).

In 1998, while still a professional player, I took up meditation, and in the next eight years or so I must have spent thousands of hours on the cushion and an equal amount of time in my study reading Buddhist literature. I was also a meditation teacher for a couple of years.

I'm often asked what the effect of meditation was on my chess and whether I would recommend it to other chess players. This is a difficult question, and only a *very* short answer or a *really* elaborate one can have any degree of validity. Having noticed that the short answer ('I don't know') is rarely found acceptable by those who ask, I have at long last decided to try my hand at an elaborate one. Hence this book.

Introduction

It's so easy to say nothing. And so true. For saying nothing *is* speaking the truth. But once it is clear that truth can never be harmed by whatever you say or don't say, it becomes easier to speak. Words can never be true, never be final, never be immune to criticism or praise. But words can *point* to the truth. In fact, they always do. When this becomes clear it is also understood that *everything* points to the truth, 'everything under the sun', to quote a well-known verse by an unknown author known as Ecclesiastes. And probably everything above the sun as well.

And so I speak. Not because what I have to say has any more truth in it than a telephone directory or a restaurant bill, but because it *is* truth. Truth, expressing itself in a way it hadn't thought of before and will never think of again. This is what truth does all the time, whether we notice it or not.

As a boy I became fascinated by chess and, gradually, almost without my noticing it, my life turned into that of a professional chess player. There I experienced both victory and defeat, much joy and much suffering, as Theodore Roosevelt puts it in a famous quote. But as I grew older, it became increasingly difficult to cope with those emotions. Victory was still fine, of course, though the formerly unknown sensation of empathy toward beaten opponents dimmed much if not all the enjoyment. Defeats started to bring with them not just the long-familiar forms of suffering (gloom, self-loathing, despair), but deep, fundamental doubts as well. Am I past my prime? Is this what the future holds: slowly spiralling downward until I'm no more than a pathetic has-been? I reached a point where the only emotionally acceptable outcome of a game was a draw. No winner, no loser, no bad feelings. But this, of course, was not very good for my professional career, which depended on my winning as many games as possible.

Then I started to meditate. Through a friend of mine who was both a chess player and a meditation teacher, I became involved with *vipassana* meditation, an ancient Buddhist practice that was then becoming popular in the West and has since firmly established itself in our culture under the new name of mindfulness. I approached meditation with the same total devotion as I had approached chess, so within a few years my self-identification as a chess player had become strongly mingled with the feeling of being a meditator and a student of Buddhism.

Did it help my chess? Maybe not, though it did make my life easier as a professional chess player in the few remaining years of my career. For though there were perhaps no significant improvements in my results, there was a marked improvement in my feeling at peace with myself, whether I won or lost. It became clear to me that it was only natural that a career as a professional sportsman, which is after all what a professional chess player is, must necessarily come to an end. A painful realization, certainly, but a natural one. Mindfulness, as I will call it from now on, helped me to end my career with only a minimum of emotional negatives. I found out that life without chess was not only possible (which was a surprise!), but actually very interesting. Many things I had pushed aside in my mind for decades were now allowed to roam free, and I became a different person in many ways. Then, a few years after I had withdrawn from chess, I quit meditation as well. Or perhaps I should say that by then I had internalized mindfulness so completely that I felt no need to continue my well-worn routine of formal meditation, which included daily sittings and several long retreats in a meditation centre each year.

Again, a new phase in my life opened up, one in which I was no longer a chess player or a practitioner of meditation. I did a lot of reflection, both on my past as a chess player and on my years on the meditation cushion. But was it reflection or was it something else? A shedding of identities, perhaps? A shift from thinking to just being aware? Reflection implies a thought process, yet thinking has strangely lost much of its former importance in my life. It's still there, of course, but somehow it no longer seems to boss me around. Nowadays, I would compare thinking to the weather. If there is bright sunshine, there is bright sunshine. If thick clouds darken the sky, then thick clouds darken the sky. If there is thinking, there is thinking. Who cares?

Yes, who cares? Or should I say: who is it that cares? That is the question this book revolves around. It is the question I dealt with in my life as a chess player and then again as a meditator. It is the question everybody has to deal with sooner or later. Who am I? What is I? Delving into this matter is an adventure with a wholly uncertain outcome. It demands courage, perhaps even desperate courage. But don't worry, it's not you who decides to take the plunge (or not). It is life itself.

Setting up the pieces

About chess

Far better is it to dare mighty things, to win glorious triumphs, even though checkered by failure, than to take rank with those poor spirits who neither enjoy much nor suffer much, because they live in the gray twilight which knows not victory nor defeat.

THEODORE ROOSEVELT

Life was pleasant in the small Dutch town where I grew up. A regional administrative and commercial centre right on the German border, Venlo had been all but destroyed during the final stages of the Second World War, but that was now a thing of the past. By the early 1960s, post-war poverty was gradually making way for affluence. There was also a change in mentality going on in these years, creating room for other than traditional lifestyles. So when I made it clear to my parents and my school teachers that I intended to take my chess seriously and that this might well result in my becoming a professional player, nobody raised any serious objections. With hindsight, I find this remarkable, given that none of the people involved had any idea what this decision actually meant, least of all myself.

But that, of course, is youth at its best: follow your star without knowing where it may take you. So when I was eighteen, I moved to Amsterdam and began a new life in the big city, the life of a chess player.

Chess is a wonderful game. It involves both struggle and beauty — the struggle to overcome your opponent and the beauty of creating something new within a strict set of rules. The rules, or, as they are sometimes called, the laws of chess, are what paint is for a painter, language for a writer, sound for a musician and any type of material for a sculptor. They set the limitations and provide the necessary stimulus to become creative. To stay within the rules, yet to somehow bend them to *your* will rather than to your opponent's will, that is the challenge. For chess is a battle of wills. Though a solitary occupation at first glance, the essence of chess is that it requires two opposing players. And that's where a game becomes something much more intimate — it becomes a fight. A fight between two brains, two minds, two personalities. But it must be a fight to the death, a gladiator fight. For only when put under the utmost pressure will a chess player find the strength to play at his very, very best. To a chess player, losing has to feel like dying. To be able to play at your best, you have to feel that you are fighting for your life.

And your opponent needs to be as serious about the game as you are, or else it won't work. I remember a game I played against my father when I was ten years old. My father was a hard-working man whose sole passion was all things technical. He disliked games, so obviously he had never played chess before. In fact, he didn't even know the rules, but for once he was in the mood to spend a little time with his son at his favourite game. Naturally, I took full advantage of this rare opportunity. He wasn't normally a patient man, but on this occasion he patiently let me explain the rules to him while playing. The result was a lot of talking, a lot of taking back of moves, and a total loss of focus on the part of the young chess player suddenly turned teacher. My father was also an intelligent and a highly practical man. To keep things as simple as possible, I hadn't explained the concept of checkmate to him. What

I *had* explained was the concept of taking your opponent's pieces. So when my father saw that I had left my king in check, he saw his chance and took it. He did so with a big smile which probably signified relief that this boring game had ended, rather than satisfaction of having won it. When I asked him for another game, he declined. I was devastated, but I accepted my loss like a good boy.

That was the only time I ever played chess with my father, and if I took anything away from that game it was that this was not chess — not to me at least. In a way it was fun; it had been an unusual moment of intimacy with my father, but it had no relation whatsoever to the game I had already come to cherish by then. Chess is real only when it is a fight between equals, a gladiator fight.

And so, at a very young age, I became a gladiator. The effect this had on my mental make-up was huge. To put it in simple terms, from now on winning would make me feel good and losing would make me feel bad. But that doesn't describe it by a long way. For when you win, you don't just feel good, you feel on top of the world. And not just on the chessboard either, but 24 hours a day. Every situation in your daily life is coloured by the self-confidence that winning can give you. When you are alone, you enjoy being alone because you are confident. If you are confident, you never feel lonely. When you are with other people, you enjoy being with them because you feel in no way inferior to them. You feel self-confident.

Until you lose. Losing destroys your self-confidence and is extremely harmful to your everyday life as well. *Now* you feel inferior to other people, lonely when you are alone and unhappy with whatever life throws at you. Winning, feeling good, self-confidence, they become a drug. When you are full of it, you feel great. When you are not, the feeling of unhappiness can be very deep.

The only consoling factor is that chess isn't just a result-oriented occupation. That's only the struggle side of it. Fortunately, chess is intensely process-oriented as well, and that is where the element of beauty comes in. Appreciating a good move, whether by yourself or by your opponent, or even by somebody else in a game that you are either watching or studying in the safety and quiet of your home, can be a fantastically rewarding experience. Finding the solution to a difficult problem in chess, even having shown and explained it to you, can be very joyful indeed. Discovering a new pattern, a new layer in the complexity of the game, a new road perhaps into what previously seemed an impenetrable chaos, is an intellectual delight. It makes you realize that your understanding of the game is growing. It makes you feel that *you* are growing, as a chess player and as a human being.

This appreciation of the beauty of chess also comes with self-confidence, but it is a slightly different form of self-confidence. The self-confidence of understanding the many complexities of chess, of being able to appreciate both its intricate patterns and its endless surprises is independent of your success (or lack of success) as a practical player. That is why there are so many people who love chess. You don't have to be a world-class player to appreciate its beauty.

About mindfulness

It is only suffering that I describe,
and the cessation of suffering.
BUDDHA

When, at the age of 42, I first walked into a meditation hall, I immediately felt this was right. For
some years I had been an avid reader of works on
philosophy and I had become especially interested
in the wisdom of the East, to be found in Hinduism, Buddhism, Taoism and other such teachings.
More often than not, these books would tell me
that it's not about learning the theory, it's about
practice. Eastern wisdom doesn't try to make you
wiser intellectually, it wants to change your life.
And now finally, here I was, in a meditation hall,
practicing. I remember vividly the excitement I
felt in these new surroundings: the Buddha stat-

ues, the soft carpet, the smell of incense. Most of all I remember the thrill of actually sitting down on a meditation cushion. How new it all was, how extraordinarily fascinating to now be a part of what I had so far only been reading about.

What first drew me to Hinduism was the *Bhagavad Gita*, an intensely compelling book that had sustained me throughout the very tough New York Open in 1995. This was a prestigious but also very exhausting chess tournament, because there were not one but two rounds a day, a very tough schedule which was (and still is) standard practice in the US, but not in Europe, where serious, high-level tournaments never exceed one game a day.

The only reason I didn't collapse was that in between games, the *Bhagavad Gita* was always there, refreshing me with its deep wisdom. I had picked it up in a local bookshop the day before the tournament, ironically more because of its slender weight and size than for any other reason. But what a surprise it turned out to be! Lines like, 'If any man thinks he slays, and if another thinks he is slain, neither knows the ways of truth. The Eternal in man cannot kill: the Eternal in man cannot die' had the most astonishing effect on me. It was enough to read one or two of these verses and then just lie on my hotel bed and allow myself to be soaked in their wisdom until the next round started. All the chess disappeared from my mind during these breaks and new energy somehow flowed back in. In fact, I didn't do anything else in New York. Just chess, the *Bhagavad Gita*, enough food and sleep to sustain me, and then back home again. I hardly noticed anything of the hustle and bustle of the big city.

When I started reading the *Tao Te Ching*, the central work of Taoism, a few years later, the effect was similar, although this time the explanation for its mysteriously healing effect was given at the very start of the book: 'The Tao that can be told is not the Tao.' Yes, this ancient text is so shrouded in mystery, yet at the same time so simple, so clear and so amazingly true, that I couldn't help but understand that it was precisely this it intended to convey: the mysterious and the straightforwardly simple are — in some incomprehensible way — exactly the same. It's like two sides of a coin: the one cannot exist without the other. One side jams the rational mind, the other side frees it. 'That which cannot be named, which cannot be spoken of, that is the Eternally Real. Naming is the beginning of existence of the myriad separate things.' I have read the book over and over again since I first laid eyes on it, and it never fails to amaze me.

Buddhism, on the other hand, seemed much more practical when I started studying it. I was struck by the wealth of spiritual exercises it offered, including many different types of meditation. The idea of working on your mind instead of just feeding it with ever new bits of information greatly appealed to me, perhaps because it was so very different from everything else I had ever done. Dimly at first, I began to see that what awaited the avid practitioner was the reward of a completely new mindset, called 'enlightenment.' Although this seemed a very unclear and faraway concept, I intuitively felt it was worthy of investigation. Most of all, perhaps it was the Buddha's promise of 'the cessation of suffering' that drew me in. As I understood it, this was inherent in enlightenment and achievable through meditation. So when I actually started to meditate, it was with the pleasurable excitement of feeling that I was on to something big. After more than twenty years of being a professional chess player, my life was taking a new turn — a peaceful one.

Since then, mindfulness has become an almost household term in the western world. But do we know what we actually mean by it? I suspect that most people will say that it is a technique, often used in therapy, to calm your mind, to help relieve stress and to improve your mental and perhaps even your physical health. While all this may be true, the mindfulness I learned was concerned with what I perceived to be a much higher goal. This, I think, was because we used to call it not mindfulness but *vipassana*. Such an ancient Asian term is naturally embedded in ancient Asian ways of thinking. For me and most of my fellow meditators, any benefits *vipassana* might bring, whether mental or physical, were no more than accidental to the ultimate Buddhist goal: 'the cessation of suffering'. It was all or nothing. Does that sound like the gladiator mentality again? Yes, it does. When I entered the meditation hall, I took my chess player's mindset with me. Of course I did.

So I started sitting (and walking, for walking meditation was just as much part of the curriculum) with one instruction only: observe, note, and let go. This applies to everything that presents itself in your meditation. The object of your attention is the breath (or, when walking, the movement of your feet), so you always start by observing the movement in your body that is caused by breathing ('in, out' or 'rising, falling'). Very soon though, I noticed that it is impossible to concentrate on breathing alone. Thoughts, emotions and physical feelings like discomfort or even pain will soon push breathing to the background.

This confused me at first, but then I began to notice that, as long as I stuck to the instruction, these phenomena behaved in exactly the same way as the rising and falling of my abdomen. The instruction is always the same: observe, note and let go. So, gradually, I learnt not to judge ('I don't like this' or 'this feels good'), and every time I did judge (which is unavoidable), to simply include the judging in my meditation: 'judging, judging').

It's easy in theory, but very hard in practice. The first time I took part in a daylong meditation retreat (by then I had got used to one-hour sessions and was beginning to have quite a high opinion of myself as a meditator), after little over an hour I fainted. This wasn't because of external circumstances being bad, because they weren't. It just showed that the mind is a wonderful thing, capable of putting up huge resistance to what it perceives as an unbearably boring way to spend a day. After all, I could equally well have gone to the beach, had a great lunch or studied chess. Fortunately, there were a few excellent teachers around, who made it clear that fainting was nothing to be worried about, so I didn't get sent packing. But my ego had suffered a direct hit.

Then there is thinking. Thoughts can be maddeningly absorbing, especially in meditation. I have had endless discussions with teachers, written books, played chess, all during meditation, all in my own mind without anybody but me noticing it. Still, to an experienced meditator, this too isn't a problem ('thinking, thinking').

Worst of all is the pain. When I started doing ten-day retreats, events where you are expected to spend the whole day meditating, which means there is no escape other than a few hours sleep and sometimes not even that, I was overwhelmed by the pain in my legs, in my back and in my whole body. This too is a trick of the mind which tells you: 'this is a terrible idea, go back home, make yourself a coffee and behave normally'. The only thing you can do (except of course to really go home) is to continue following the one and only instruction for mindfulness: observe, note, and let go. And sure enough, after living in pain for days, continually changing my meditation posture without finding relief for more than a few minutes, the pain became less intense and finally even disappeared for short periods. In my later retreats, it even disappeared entirely. This made me very happy indeed and almost caused me to think that I had reached the 'cessation of suffering', a plausible thought for someone who no longer suffers.

But that wasn't the whole story, for most of the meditation teachers I met told me that 'observing, noting and letting go of' the phenomena, difficult as it was, was not enough. It was necessary to see in them the three characteristics of all existence, formulated in ancient Pali texts such as *Dukkha*, *Aniccia* and *Anattā*, roughly translated as Suffering, Impermanence, and No-Self. This I knew, but not for a moment had I managed to identify these characteristics in my meditation practice. Sure, when I sat there with an agonizing pain in my back, the element of suffering was overwhelmingly and undeniably there. To be aware of this didn't require any great wisdom. But although in these moments I was practically praying for the impermanence of pain to manifest itself, impermanence never showed up when I really needed it. And No-Self, though very intriguing as a concept, was never more to me than that: just another concept. Not for a moment was I ever aware of it in my meditation. So seeing the three characteristics of all existence? Not me.

What then was the point of this ancient Buddhist teaching, which none of my Buddhist teachers were ever able to explain to my satisfaction? Looking back, I can now see that they actually showed great wisdom in not being able to explain, for such questions cannot be answered. They can only dissolve. And for that to happen, one needs to journey on. So I went on a journey, a long journey that took me from mindfulness to no-mind and then to 'never mind'. But was it a journey? Or was it just a change of perspective?

About the unknowable

Life is not a task. There is absolutely nothing
to attain except the realization that there is
absolutely nothing to attain.

TONY PARSONS

So far I had always been working towards a goal
in my life. First at school, where I always aimed
at being top of my class, then for many long
years in chess, where trying to be the best was
essential to playing the game at a high level, and
finally, though I had not been aware of it, in meditation.

Of course, meditation itself contains no el-
ements of competition or trying to be the best,
but if competitiveness is firmly anchored in your
mind, it will always be present in your meditation practice as well. Since I was a diligent stu-

dent by nature, it was only natural for me to do my best, and since I was also an ambitious person by nature, I naturally set my sights high in whatever I did, including meditation. Enlightenment, the cessation of suffering — I wasn't intending to settle for anything less.

There is nothing wrong with this attitude, but it does tend to keep your mind focused on the future, for a goal necessarily always lies in the future. Mindfulness, on the other hand, is about being in the present. Not because there is anything wrong with thinking about either the past or the future, but because when meditating there is simply just one thing for you to do: observe, note, and let go. So thinking about a goal or whatever else may await you in the future automatically gets reduced to just thinking ('thinking, thinking') and nothing else. You don't follow the thinking to its conclusion, you don't get excited by it; you just observe it and let it go. Internalizing this strategy, this attitude towards whatever life throws at you, cannot help but make thought processes lighter, less overbearing in your mind. It also means that thinking gets diverted from its usual channels. It becomes rather like looking into a mirror. Not an ordinary mirror, which shows what you expect to see, but a magical one, which shows things from a different perspective.

This is the perspective (for want of a better word) of nonduality.

Like mindfulness, Zen and many other such 'spiritual' terms, all relatively new to the languages of the West, nonduality is a rather fashionable word that is often used as a way to say exactly nothing at all. That may not sound very positive, but in a strange twist of irony this is precisely what it is intended to say, for nonduality is a word for showing up the 'other side' of duality, which is our normal way of looking at things. We need to distinguish things to be able to see them, talk about them. This glass of water here is different from that painting over there. I am me, living *my* unique life, and you are you, living *your* unique life. These clear distinctions between people, things, places and moments in time are practical tools that we use to deal with the world. In fact, without them there would *be* no world. And that, of course, would be absurd.

Yet it is precisely here, in this area of absurdity, that nonduality enters the scene.

By exposing our seemingly rock-solid reality as just a convention, a practical tool, a trick of the mind if you like, the absurd and the normal are shown to be just two sides of one and the same coin. The coin of oneness.

Our life, our way of experiencing ourselves, is

based on the assumption that it is happening to *us*. That is the perspective of common sense: very sane, very sensible and something that everybody will agree on. It is also the perspective of duality. But take 'us' away and what is left? Life, just life. An ever-changing ('impermanence') stream of experiences that when taken personally alternately makes us happy or unhappy ('suffering'). But only because we take it personally! *I* am alive, so *I* suffer, which is a problem for *me*. This is what the practice of mindfulness will eventually expose. What we call reality is built on the cornerstone of *me*. Take that cornerstone away ('no-self') and the building collapses.

To *me* that sounds like a frightening prospect, but the thing is that when this collapse happens, the *me* isn't there. And without *me* being there to get frightened, the collapse is frightening nobody.

The concept of nonduality isn't a concept. Understanding it has no relevance, it's not even possible. Just like mindfulness reduces all conceptual thinking in meditation to a mere 'thinking, thinking', the non-concept of nonduality reduces everything to nothing at all. I had had glimpses of this reality-beyond-reality before, but it all came together when in 2004 I started attending occasional meetings by Tony Parsons, an Englishman whose teaching (or non-teaching) is neatly summarized by the title of one of his books: *Nothing being everything*. Nothing, the unknowable, the unqualified 'this', *is* being, and in being *is* everything. Yes, it is a paradox. But it is only in paradoxes that such things can be talked about.

If the above sounds a bit too theoretical, too vague, or too whatever, it is because these are only words and, as I said before, words don't mean a thing. They only point. But if to you they seem to point to nothing at all, I can only say 'Yes! That's it, that's it exactly.' Thinking never clarifies the truth, it obscures it. Even just *seeing* the truth obscures it. Truth is not something that can be understood or seen, it's what *is*. Now, here, in this moment, is truth and nothing but truth. It cannot be defined, cannot be grasped. It's the unknowable. The unknowable is Now.

This is the great non-teaching of no-self, non-duality, or whatever it is called by those who know yet don't know. Tony Parsons calls it The Open Secret, but he also sometimes calls it marmalade. Hinduism tells us that life as we know it is really a game, a divine game, played by the gods.

A game, not a serious business, and yet the most serious thing in the world, the *only* thing in the world — does that remind me of chess? Well, perhaps it does. Perhaps I did 'get' this because chess had already taught me this paradoxical truth many years before. A game and a serious business, they are each other's opposites only in the world of logic, i.e. in duality. Look at the other side of the coin and such distinctions simply aren't there anymore.

The Opening

Getting hooked

The excitement of playing a chess tournament can be very powerful. It's the sort of power that can lift you up so high that when it puts you down again you find yourself on a totally different plane than where you were before. You may even find yourself to be a different person. It is impossible to say when I first felt this, but two memories stand out in this respect.

One is the first tournament I ever played, the junior championship of my hometown Venlo, when I was thirteen. It lasted a whole weekend, which was an eternity to me at the time, and I had to wrestle permission from my parents to skip Holy Mass on Sunday morning before I was allowed to enter. The organization was pretty informal judged by my later professional standards, but it was a far cry from the childishness and chaos

of the school events that constituted my only previous experience with 'organized' chess. This was
a real tournament! There were no age categories
back then, and I was the youngest participant.
Naturally, this was a bit intimidating to start with,
but it proved highly stimulating later on, when
it turned out I could actually beat most of these
older boys and girls. The climax came on day
two, when I faced the two strongest players in the
field, both five years older than I, and beat them
both. I was beside myself with joy for winning
these games, but the real treasure was the rapture
I felt *during* these games, the way I felt myself unexpectedly and incomprehensibly performing at
a much higher level than I ever had before. I felt
quite literally uplifted to heights which I hadn't
even known existed. We played with a thirty-min-
ute time limit (no increment in those days!) and
didn't write down our moves. I remember that I
played the Vienna Opening against both of them.
I remember that I manoeuvred my king's knight
via e2 and g3 to f5 to great effect in both games,
but I don't have any scoresheets. I finished third
behind these two eighteen-year-olds, because my
slow start on day one saddled me with too great a
handicap to overcome even with a perfect finish.
Still, I don't think that winning the event could
have made me any happier than I was.

The only disappointment was my prize, because it was a money prize, and I didn't want money, I wanted a trophy! So the next day I took my money to a trophy shop and bought myself a tiny trophy without an inscription, which was all I could afford. Apart from a very inaccurate newspaper cutting, I have no other memorabilia of this tournament. But the trance-like experience, the thrill of it, and the feeling of coming home a different boy, are things I have never forgotten.

I suppose I was hooked then and there, and I never had a chance to *not* become a chess player after this experience. But my fate was definitely sealed after my next 'big' tournament, which was the provincial junior championship almost a year later. This was completely new territory for me, so, as with the Venlo championship, I just felt tremendously excited and had no expectation of achieving any sort of result at all. But it happened again! No sooner had the tournament begun than I felt myself transformed into a different person, as if somewhere in me there was an expert chess player who took over the moment the clocks were started. On day one were the preliminaries, and I just beat these guys, who were all older than I was. In every game I felt raised to a level where my opponents just couldn't touch me.

But day two proved more complicated, for

now that I was in the final, it dawned on me that I had something to lose. This realization was new to me, and I was almost overcome by an emotion I had never felt at a chessboard before: fear. For the first time in my life, I was playing under the watchful eyes of a crowd that had become interested in this little boy overnight, and I felt a terrible fear that I might not be able to live up to the expectations. Fortunately, however, the fear didn't undermine my concentration. Quite the contrary, in fact, for a tremendously strong determination rose in me not to lose, not to make any mistakes. Looking back, it seems to me that on this day, young as I was, the gladiator in me was born. I understood that I might easily lose all my games to these finalists, who were the strongest players in the tournament, and I didn't want that to happen. I *really* didn't want that to happen, I didn't want to die. And so I didn't. I fought for my life, and though I lacked the power to win games, I did find the strength not to lose any. There were four rounds in the final, and I drew all of them, which at the time was an unprecedented feat for such a young and inexperienced player. Of course, this didn't win me the championship (I came third — again!), but I was very, very happy to have remained undefeated. There was no trophy this time, nor any money to buy one, but I didn't care. The tournament had been a great success, and I had discovered a new quality in myself. I could hold my own in a tense tournament situation against very strong opposition. The stronger the better, in fact. Somewhere in me lingered a fighting spirit that could only be awakened when the stakes were high, very high. Survival instinct? Or was it something for which the words came only much later in my life: an experience of no-self? Whatever it was, like in my first tournament, I came home a different boy.

These were the first of many such experiences, although, to be fair, they remained the exception rather than the rule. In my 'normal' state of mind, I didn't believe in miracles, and so they didn't happen. Even then, I was a good player who achieved results that were good enough to build a professional career on. But in the back of my mind there was always this longing for such 'highs' to manifest themselves again.

So perhaps, looking back, I must admit that it wasn't so much chess itself I had got hooked on, it was these peak experiences that chess gave me from time to time. When, in my late thirties, such experiences became less frequent as well as less intense, chess began to lose much of its appeal. This wasn't helped by the realization that I was slowly being pushed aside by a new generation. I started to feel old, especially when I began to rec-ognize my former self in these youngsters. Not surprisingly, all this caused me considerable suf-fering. Since, by that time, I had read quite a lot of Eastern philosophy, it was perhaps only natural that I should turn for help to Buddhism, which so plainly offered it.

Help!

There are many legends surrounding the origins of Buddhism. Whether any of these come even remotely close to what really happened all those thousands of years ago will probably never be known. But what comes across very clearly from the multitude of legends, traditions, stories and teachings that are all sheltered under that magnificent umbrella called Buddhism, is the desire to help. Buddhism provides deep theoretical frameworks for the intellect, age-old rituals and a strong sense of community for the soul, and many forms of meditation for those who feel the need to *do* something.

For that is what meditation is: *doing* something. It is ironic that to an outsider meditating looks like doing exactly nothing at all, since the truth is that it is actually very, very hard work.

At least, that is what I gradually found out. At first, the practicalities of meditation did not seem so very different from chess. You go to a certain place, you practice for a fixed period of time, and when it is all over you can relax, go home and do all the things you're used to doing. But that is only the beginning. I was taken out of my initial mindfulness-comfort zone when I first signed up for a whole day. Three things happened to me that day that made a lasting impression on me.

The first I have already mentioned earlier in this book: after an hour or so, while standing upright in between sitting and walking meditation, I felt myself losing consciousness and slowly collapsing onto the floor. Why and how this happened is not really relevant, but I suspect that my mind wanted to make a clear statement about what I was doing ('No to this crap!').

Secondly, I experienced an awful lot of pain. Pain in my legs, in my back, and finally in my whole body. When discussing our experiences with the whole group at the end of the day, I was relieved to hear from other first-time participants that they had had the same experience. A woman of about my age said it had been worse than the pain of giving birth.

Thirdly, on going home I didn't take the tram as I usually did, but I went on foot — a walk of almost two hours, which was not something I was used to doing at the time. But after a whole day of meditation, I felt so wonderfully energized, so happy, so free, that taking a long, unhurried walk seemed the most natural thing in the world to do. Whether this was indeed one of the benefits of the meditation or whether it was a manifestation of the sheer joy that the ordeal was over, I don't know, but it was a great feeling, and it added strongly to the idea that it had been a very special day.

About half a year later, I did my first ten-day meditation retreat. This again seemed similar to a chess tournament to start with, but oh what a difference it turned out to be! The retreat was held in a meditation centre in a leafy suburb of a small town not far from Amsterdam. When I got out of my car I thought, wow, what a great place to hold a chess tournament, so quiet and peaceful! But when I saw the very basic room that was to be mine for the duration of the retreat I began to feel uneasy. It had been many years ago that I had accepted anything less than a comfortable, modern hotel room when playing a chess tournament. This took me back quite a few years and many steps on the comfort ladder. No mini-bar, no television, no reading material (one of the rules of the retreat), nothing! Nothing of interest, that is, nothing to take away our focus from what we had come there to do: non-stop meditation from early in the morning until late at night.

In all honesty, I can only say that this first meditation retreat was hell. The pain was horrible, my motivation wavered to the point of disappearing, and the thought of being no good at this became totally predominant in my mind. The breaking point came on day three. I went to the teacher to tell her I was leaving. She was a woman in her late sixties, a very gentle creature and an experienced meditator. She was also someone with a great love of people. Her answer was, 'Of course you may leave, Paul, but I don't think it's necessary. Why don't you go for a little walk first and decide afterwards?' This surprised me for two reasons. One was her saying it wasn't 'necessary'. That suggested that *she* didn't consider me unfit for meditation at all. Had she seen things in me that I was unaware of myself? Was I perhaps not the hopeless case I thought I was? Second, the idea of 'going for a little walk' struck me as breaking the rules of the retreat, for that was precisely what we were not supposed to do. The one basic rule of a mindfulness retreat is to never stop observing, noting and letting go, whatever happens, and so far I had taken this very literally. But when I did go out for a walk, I immediately noticed that I wasn't breaking the mindfulness at all. Yes, it was nice to be outside, it was pleasant to see 'normal' people and flowers and trees again, but all the time I was walking, I was in fact continuing the meditation. After about twenty minutes, I went back, told the teacher I wasn't leaving until tomorrow and carried on where I had left off. During the remainder of the retreat, I was always able to delay my departure until 'tomorrow' just by reminding myself that I was free to leave whenever I wanted. When I told the teacher about this little trick, she just smiled and said no more about it. I guess she knew all about such mind games. In the end, of course, tomorrow never came. When the ten days were over, I was immensely proud to have persevered, and very grateful to the teacher, who had managed to stop me from leaving — and with so little effort! To stop someone from leaving by giving him permission to leave — it sounds almost absurd, but what an effective method it had been in my case!

Perhaps it was then that somewhere in the back of my mind I started thinking: I also want to be able to do this, I also want to help others discover the power of mindfulness.

The power of mindfulness. Around the same time that I did my first ten-day retreat, Eckhart Tolle's bestseller *The Power of Now* became popular. In this, his first book, Tolle not only describes the inner transformation he had undergone, but he also invents a vocabulary of his own in order to be able to talk about it. The same teacher who led my first retreat (and most of my later ones as well) recommended this book. I read it and was struck by the similarity of Tolle's *Power of Now* and 'our' power of mindfulness. It then struck me again that this is perhaps also what is meant by enlightenment in Buddhism.

This I found rather confusing. Wasn't enlightenment something to be attained, something that might be the *result* of mindfulness, not mindfulness itself? It would be a few years before it gradually dawned on me that the whole idea of 'attaining enlightenment' is precisely what makes enlightenment so unattainable. The power of Now consists in Now being all there is. The power of mindfulness is the same, because in mindfulness, 'now' is the only thing that *is* real. Nowadays, mindfulness is usually presented as a method to improve ourselves, to solve our problems and make our lives better. But while this may be true, the actual mechanics of the 'improvement' are very different from what you would expect. While sitting with all the things you want to change, the shift in focus gradually changes from these 'things' to mindfulness itself, from the outside world to the here and now. And that changes everything.

It's like being instructed to go to the left in order to go to the right. It's not logical. But mindfulness has a habit of dissolving logic, as it dissolves everything that crosses its path ('observing, noting, letting go'). Such is the power of mindfulness.

So, logic, that powerful tool that forms the bedrock of all our thinking, turns out to be not the ruler of the universe after all. But that's not logical, so by thinking alone (which is letting logic reign supreme) this can never be seen. In mindfulness, however, where thinking is always just 'thinking, thinking', the shift in focus comes naturally. You can't stop it.

Logic

In chess, logic is everything. That's why humans are so good at it and computers even better. 'If I play *this*, he must reply *thus,* and then I've got him: checkmate!' That's the standard pattern of thought for any chess player. The better you are at extending this formula in width and depth, the better a player you will be. But you will never be a match for a computer that is able to extend its 'thinking' powers almost *ad infinitum.*

I was lucky enough to be born some forty years before the computer began to teach us, humans, that greatest of all virtues: humility. In fact, the end of my career as a competitive chess player practically coincided with the beginning of the computer era in chess as well as in daily life. Thus, I was never faced with the cruel new reality of a chess player's mind being dwarfed by a computer. This is what makes life so very different for today's chess professionals from what it was like for my generation and the generations before me. When 'we' won, 'we' were simply the best, no discussion. Back in 1990, I was able to play a simul against 24 computers, and I beat them: 13½-10½. Nowadays, this has become an unthinkable feat. Even world champions, after their games are over, humbly ask the 'engines' to tell them where they could have played better. And they do. The engines are always right, no discussion.

Chess is a game of logic, but it's also such a complex game that the logic of it is not always easily understood. That's what makes chess difficult. The ability to find the logic in seemingly illogical moves is what distinguishes a great chess player from an average one. But there is also the element of beauty. The possibility of *understanding* the logic behind great moves played by great players is what makes chess a wonderful game, even for those who wouldn't be able to find these moves for themselves (or wouldn't dare play them if they did). Admiring the games of top players is one way of enjoying the beauty of chess, and a very important one.

An experienced chess player must therefore necessarily be a logical thinker. In fact, this is one of the reasons why chess is often presented as an educational tool. When you start playing chess, you automatically start thinking logically, even if you've never done it before. This is learning by playing, not by being taught. When you play chess, you just can't help but develop your capacity for logical thinking, whether you want to or not.

So what's wrong with logic? Well, nothing, of course, just as there is nothing wrong with thinking in general. But the more a meditator gets used to being mindful, the more he will be living not in his thoughts, but in the moment. This shift in perspective is an automatic one. When you start practicing mindfulness, you just can't help developing your 'capacity' for being mindful. Thinking has nothing to do with it. Even worse (from the perspective of logic), thinking will be gradually seen through as fundamentally different from being mindful. Thinking becomes subordinated to mindfulness.

That is why, in all my years as a meditator, I was never consciously aware of any personal problems I might have solved by meditation. It is also why I never noticed any progress on my 'way to enlightenment.' With mindfulness, problems have a habit of solving themselves, and they don't care if you notice them disappearing or not. As for the 'way to enlightenment,' that concept (for that's what it is) is just another of the many things that get reduced to 'thinking, thinking' in mindfulness. Some day you may find that it just isn't there anymore.

In mindfulness, *all* concepts lose their power. Deconstructing them or even thinking them over isn't necessary. Like old soldiers, they simply fade away.

Of course, all this suggests that mindfulness isn't necessarily the best of tools for a chess player to have. But this, I think, is an unanswerable question. The effects of mindfulness on the mind of an elite chess player will be different in each individual case. What I am fairly confident of, though, is that mindfulness will benefit the human being *behind* the chess player in the long run. And although many a chess player has long forgotten that *au fond* he or she *is* a human being, one day it will come back to them. It did in my case. And though the realization was a bit scary at first, it made for an excellent start in my post-chess life.

Being in control

The better you are at chess, the stronger your sense of control will be. Especially during a very successful period, when you win a lot of games, perhaps even tournaments, the feeling of being in control can be very strong indeed. And this is wonderful. In fact, it is one of the great rewards of being successful in anything, not only chess.

The downside, of course, is that when you have an *un*successful period, the feeling of having *lost* control can be equally strong. And this can be truly devastating, since chess players can lose confidence very quickly and this makes a big difference to their playing strength. I remember all too well those tournaments where I fell into a losing streak and just couldn't get out of it, no matter how hard I tried. It's like a disease. You can't shrug it off. It has to wear itself out or be cured.

That tournament in Tallinn in 1987, for instance, where, after having lost four games in a row, I just knew that I was going to lose my last-round game as well, even though my opponent was not a particularly dangerous player. The same happened in a small qualification tournament for a place on the 1980 Dutch Olympic team. This was even more embarrassing, since I lost *all* my games (though admittedly the total number was less than in Tallinn — only four).

This is one of the reasons why, if you want to be a good chess player over an extended period, and certainly as a professional, you have to constantly keep improving. You just need that exhilarating feeling of being successful, of getting better, of reaching new heights, of climbing higher and higher. It is a necessary confirmation of that ultimately important feeling of being in control. Paradoxically, this implies that underneath the surface, the feeling of *not* being good enough (no matter how good you are) is a constant companion, invisible perhaps for most of the time, but always on the lookout for an opportunity to grab you. New successes are constantly needed in order to suppress this haunting insecurity.

That is why many chess players lose their inner drive after they have reached the pinnacle of what they think they can achieve. At least two world champions, Paul Morphy in the nineteenth and Bobby Fischer in the twentieth century, retired soon after achieving their ultimate goal. Having beaten every rival in the world, the fire within them had simply burned itself out. Personally, I never 'recovered' from reaching the Candidates Matches in 1993. Although I went on playing professionally for another eight years — and sustained a fairly decent level until the end — I always knew that this had been the high point of my career, the pinnacle of what was achievable for me, and that from now on there was only one way left for me and that was downhill.

The fact that self-confidence plays such a large part in a chess player's performance strongly suggests a close relationship between chess and mental fitness. In order to be successful in chess, it is not enough to have the *potential* to play well, you have to actually *perform*. Talent, understanding and knowledge are only the beginning. What is at least as important is the will to win, the determination to give it your all. This is a state of mind that is not always there when you need it.

Many of today's top players are fully aware of how important the mental element is, and they work with psychologists. For me and most of my contemporaries, this 'luxury' didn't exist. The few of us who did have an inkling of how vital the mental element in chess is, had to work it all out by themselves. I was lucky enough to be able to discuss these things with my wife, who, though not a psychologist, has enough understanding of human nature — and of chess — to realize that this was indeed crucial to my becoming a better player (and probably a more contented husband as well). One of our early successes came in 1981, when we made a plan to overcome my fear of a then fellow-International Master, against whom I had a disastrous score even though we had been of approximately equal strength for some time. He was what we call in Dutch an 'Angstgegner', a German word to denote someone to whom you have lost several games in the past and to whom you are afraid of losing again in the future. We decided that, when at home, I was to say aloud, clearly audible and with full conviction, 'I am at least as strong as X', to be repeated several times a day, until X and I would meet again. It worked! I beat him for the first time ever, the spell was broken and from then on we played on an equal footing. I still lost to him from time to time, but I also won a lot of games. The balance had been restored.

Much later, when I became interested in philosophy, I was helped by the radical notion of *struggle* (in all forms) being a crucial aspect of human existence. The ancient Greek philosopher

Heraclitus, for instance, with his central theme of *constant change* and his famous saying 'War is the father of all things', made a tremendous impression on me. I knew that struggle had also been a central theme in the philosophy of Emanuel Lasker, the only chess player who had been both a World Champion — the longest reigning ever, no less, from 1894 until 1921 — and a serious philosopher. Somehow this felt like a confirmation that studying philosophy could help me in my efforts to become a better chess player. It wasn't just a better opening repertoire I needed; seeing chess in its proper perspective, both philosophically and psychologically, was also important. I felt it would make me more complete, both as a chess player and as a human being. From there it was only a small step to becoming interested in Buddhism, with its central notion of human suffering and its proposed way of ending the suffering.

Mindfulness has its own way of dealing with the feeling of being (or not being) in control. I can tell you that a relentless treatment with the method of 'observing, noting, and letting go' wears down everything in the end, even a thought as strong and as fundamental to your idea of who you are as the notion of 'you being in control'. Once you sit down and start meditating, the idea of being in control will eventually get dissected into its constituent parts of *Aniccia, Dukkha* and *Anattā,* just like everything else. It may then disappear altogether before coming back into focus again as something like 'yes, of course, that's what I used to call my feeling of being in control, how funny!'

So there we have them again, *Aniccia, Dukkha* and *Anattā,* those three mysterious, ancient Pali terms that I was never actually aware of in my meditation. But the truth is they are simply there, always, whether anyone sees them or not. *Aniccia,* or Impermanence, can be made to sound a little more 'western' and homely if you translate it into Heraclitus' 'Change is the only Constant'. Paradoxical, perhaps, but very rational as well.

Dukkha, or Suffering, is definitely not the first idea that comes to mind when you are feeling in control of things. But once you have experienced the feeling of *not* being in control and the helplessness that comes with it, that may change. And it is precisely this element of change, the instability of the feeling that you are in control, that makes the *Dukkha* visible even in everything that is bright and wonderful. Even the loveliest moments of my life are *Dukkha* just *because* they are *Aniccia.*

All this may come across as rather discouraging, but it is the third characteristic, *Anattā,* that is the liberating ingredient in the cocktail. Once you realize that the notion of a separate self, a 'me' that is either in control or not in control of 'my' life, is just an idea, a thought like so many others that come and go as they please (not as pleases me), a long pent-up feeling of freedom *may* be released and sweep away the 'me' and everything that goes with it. It might then be clear — to nobody! — that 'we' have only adopted the idea of 'self' in our early youth for reasons of expediency. Our parents would have been greatly disappointed if we hadn't learned to communicate on the basis of you and me. But it has no more basis in truth than Santa Claus or the things we dream. *Anattā* means freedom for the 'I', because there *is* no 'I'. I am free because I'm not there.

It is a long story and it takes a lot of believing if you only read about it and don't have the first-hand experience. You have to see it for yourself, or else it will be just words, just another concept, and therefore not real. Mindfulness is the app in your mind that will see this, but since no two minds are alike, the app works differently for every living being. There is no user guide. Meditation is one way of activating it, but there is really no saying how it works for *you*. Truth never hides, but thinking is fond of obscuring it.

Nothing won, nothing lost

So how does the absence of a me-that-is-in-control work out for a chess player? What does it mean in practice? Is it to my advantage? To my disadvantage? Let me be mercilessly clear about this: it makes no difference whatsoever. This is for the very simple reason that there never *was* a me-that-is-in-control. It was always just an idea, never reality. Even when you still thought you were in control, you weren't. This is illustrated by the famous ancient Zen saying: 'before enlightenment, chop wood and carry water; after enlightenment, chop wood and carry water.' For a chess player this translates as: 'before enlightenment, win and lose; after enlightenment, win and lose.' But the 'me' has gone out of it and *that* makes a world of difference. Life, including chess, becomes so much lighter without a 'me' doing things.

The unbearable lightness of being? Perhaps. But if we put it like this, it is important to add that the lightness is unbearable for no one.

Naturally though, on a personal level, there will be differences. Although there is no I, all living beings have their own characteristics. No one person is a carbon copy of another. In choosing to try meditation, I was greatly influenced by my first teacher, who was a friend as well as an excellent chess player himself. Eight years my senior, he had a freshness, an energy, and a fearlessness in his chess that never seemed to wilt, even when he grew older. I never discussed this with him, but somehow I took it for granted that his success as a chess player was in large part due to the fact that he had been meditating intensively for many years. Perhaps I expected a similar positive effect on *my* chess when *I* started meditating. But it never came... still, if it is true that meditation is beneficial, it must also be true that what is good for you when you're just starting out is totally different from what is good for you when your career is drawing to a close. He had started in his early twenties, while I was already forty-two when I first sat on a meditation cushion. Also, our personalities were different, his was a much more energetic and confident one. It would have been weird if the effects *had* been the same.

There is a certain irony in the fact that we are both called Paul. For Paul 1, who started to meditate when he was young, one of the many effects of meditation was probably that it helped him to be the fearless attacking player that he naturally was. For Paul 2, who started to meditate when he was about twenty years older than Paul 1 had been, meditation helped him to say goodbye to his lifelong passion when the time had come to do so.

So, superficially, meditation had diametrically opposite effects on the two Pauls. But on a deeper level, the effect on both of us was exactly the same: it brought us what we needed most.

Was it with the intention of restoring my chess to its former glory that I took up meditation in 1998? It is always tricky to answer such questions about one's past, but I'm fairly certain that it wasn't my chess that I thought needed restoration. It was my life. For when you find what was once your grand passion being slowly transformed into something more akin to a drab routine, then this affects much more than just your chess.

But isn't this what is usually called a midlife crisis? And doesn't this happen to almost everybody sooner or later in life? A Buddhist might congratulate you and tell you that the eternal truth of Impermanence (*Aniccia*) has finally been revealed to you, that naturally this causes severe Suffering (*Dukkha*), and that this suffering can only be counteracted by the realization of No-Self (*Anattā*). A modern psychotherapist will probably tell you the same, but in a different language.

It may sound like the height of idiocy, and yes, it is a mystery, a paradox, a miracle and so much more, but it is only when there is no self that you are truly yourself. There is a relaxing into whatever the moment has to offer. Ideas about your past or future do not disappear, but they become less dominating. They don't boss you around any longer. In fact, they never did. How could they when there *is* no 'you' to be bossed around?

So what happened to me when I gave up chess? Well, first of all, I gave up only the part of the professional and competitive *player*. The love of the game itself remained, although I did need a few years of total abstention from chess before I discovered this. But once I had grown accustomed to a life without the thrills, the satisfaction, the stress and the distress that are an integral part of a chess player's existence, the pure love of the game that had always lain beneath these emotional storms made itself felt again. Since then, I have been an enthusiastic writer about the game and also an avid fan of today's elite players, whose games I follow online as often as I can.

My life has become much more quiet, more relaxed and more oriented toward the present moment. Thoughts about past and present are still there, of course, but even while I enjoy or hate them, they are always seen for what they are: just thoughts, nothing serious. Most of all, however, the idea that this is indeed 'my life' has been turned on its head. The famous Shakespeare quote 'to be or not to be, that is the question' has met its match in 'to be, yet not to be, that is the answer'.

In other words: this thing called 'my life', is it reality or is it a dream? I cannot put this any clearer than by saying that it is and it isn't.

This is the teaching of nonduality. But it isn't a teaching. It isn't a separate creed either. This is not the spiritual property of one philosophy, one religion, or one man alone. On the contrary, nonduality can be found everywhere. Literally *everywhere*. But perhaps it is precisely for this reason that it is always overlooked. We can't see the air that we breathe either.

Nonduality, the black hole

Like every other human being, a chess player lives in a dualistic world, a world where distinctions matter. 'I am I and you are you, what's mine is mine and what's yours is yours (and whoever tells me otherwise is mad).' In truth, this view of the world is a necessary tool for any person to be able to live in it. It is only when the person questions his being a person that every other tool in his toolkit gets questioned as well. But this doesn't usually happen until the 'person' is forced or tempted into an extreme situation, where the concentration on Now becomes so overpowering that there is simply no room left for anything else. This Now is like a black hole, where the force of gravity is so strong that nothing can escape from it.

If there is one place where chess and medita-tion meet, it is in this black hole, this intense concentration on Now. Every serious chess player has had moments when the necessity of mobilizing *all* his mental powers and focusing them on one point and one point only, was of vital importance to stay in the game. Every serious meditator has also reached this point, albeit via a different route. It has been my privilege to have followed both routes and to have recognized that no matter which road you take, the Power of Now (thank you, Eckhart Tolle!) is always there, always ready to blow your preconceived ideas about yourself and about the world out of the water.

This is no secret. The truth of it can be found everywhere. In fact, I am often impressed by the many different ways in which great artists express it. Franz Kafka, for instance, wrote in his diary that it was his dearest wish to develop a world view (*and* the ability to put it in writing, so as to convince others) wherein life retains its natural progression but is seen at the same time, and just as clearly, as a nothing, a dream, a state of uncertainty. There are countless other examples. The Power of Now, which is also the power of mindfulness, cannot be caught in words, but whenever someone tries to catch it anyway, the attempt never fails to move me.

When I was still a professional chess player, I had many glimpses of this, but it was only after I started to meditate that my mind began to open up to the completely different perspective from which these glimpses originate. Perhaps I first discovered a direct link between chess and mindfulness in late 1999, when I was preparing one of my games for publication. To my own great surprise, I suddenly found myself making an inspired attempt to describe the deep unity that I felt between me and my opponent, leaving all chess jargon aside:

'For there was no death, no killer. No winner, no loser. We were one and eternal, and when after the concluding moves my opponent resigned, the overpowering impression wasn't so much that I had won the game, but that what had been was no more.

Nothing remained,
no struggle,
no arena,
no chess.

And yet, there was nothing
that wasn't there.'

Paradoxically, since I have learned to recognize these glimpses for what they are, they have become few and far between. Perhaps the realization that *every* moment is a special moment has obliterated the specialness of the 'special' moments. Perhaps there is another reason. But the truth is that questions beginning with 'why' have lost much of their interest. Sure, when Magnus Carlsen manages to pull off another incredible win, I try to figure out how he does these things time and time again. Chess remains a game of logic, a dualistic struggle between two players. It will always invite dualistic thinking. But the position of duality itself has changed. It now knows its proper place. And that place is that of a game, a dance, a way for unknowable and invisible nonduality to manifest itself und thus become knowable and visible. Knowable and visible to itself. That is to say: to us, whether we actually see it or not. Life just goes on, and what happened is not a big deal. Even when it is, it still isn't.

The Middlegame

Boredom and loneliness

One of the first so-called obstacles I met in my meditation practice, apart from the physical pain, was boredom. 'Obstacle' in this context is a technical term for a certain category of unpleasant experiences that no meditator will be able to avoid and is likely to cause serious motivation problems. This is what happened to me during my first retreat, when, as I described earlier, the pain and my inability to cope with it convinced me that I was no good as a meditator and that I'd better quit and do something useful instead. The obstacle had done its work: I couldn't go on — or so I thought. What the teacher then did was something I didn't understand at the time, but which I find very revealing in hindsight. She told me it wasn't *necessary* for me to leave. It was just that I had encountered a typical obstacle: pain.

And the pain was telling me something: 'Paul! Look at me!' The pain *wanted* to be faced, and so far I hadn't really done that, I had only endured. But to endure an obstacle is not enough, or perhaps I should say it's not *vipassana*. To endure is the way of willpower, not of mindfulness. To just sit with the pain and face it, or, as the *vipassana* instruction says — observe, note and let go — this I hadn't done yet, at least not properly.

Though the pain had been both frightening and discouraging during that first retreat, the experience had been fascinating and — inexplicably perhaps — I soon found that I wanted more of it. So I quickly signed up for a second retreat, and then for a third, and so on and so on. In fact, it was very much the same as it had been with chess: somehow or other I just got hooked.

It was probably during my third retreat that the pain gradually lessened. Whether this was the result of me following instructions better, the pain wearing itself out, or some other reason, I don't know. But I enjoyed it — for a short time only, because to my intense surprise, room was immediately made for other 'problems' to emerge. The first of these was boredom.

When you meditate for hours and hours, possibly even days or weeks on end, you just cannot help getting bored sooner or later. It is a logical result of being in a situation where you are deprived of all of your usual stimulants. In a retreat (a proper *vipassana* retreat that is) there is no tv, no smartphone, no internet, no coffee, no alcohol, no ordinary human contact, no nothing. Nothing, that is, to divert you from your meditation, or, to put it more bluntly, nothing to divert you from what goes on inside your mind. You are alone with yourself.

But while I wasn't used to feeling pain, boredom was nothing new to me. As a chess player who often travelled to places without any distractions and sometimes had to stay there for weeks, I was used to boredom and loneliness.

Not that I had enjoyed those tournaments in the middle of nowhere. But what they had taught me was that being lonely and bored wasn't *necessarily* a bad thing. Sure, in tournaments where there was little else to do but wait for the next round, there had always been a fine line between falling into a depression and keeping my energy level up. This would usually depend on my results. As long as I played well, I could concentrate on what I had come there to do: to play chess. But whenever things went badly, my self-confidence would drop to levels where boredom and loneliness could easily tip me over the edge and trigger a depression. Losing my last five games in tournaments in Baku and Tallinn, both still in the days of Soviet isolation from all things fun, desirable, western and decadent, came as a direct result of such moments of total collapse.

But it didn't always go wrong. There was this tournament in Albena, a holiday resort on the Bulgarian Black Sea coast, where I played fairly well, exceeding my own expectations in fact, even though for two whole weeks there had been just one other player I was on friendly terms with and swimming and sunbathing were my only recreations. Admittedly, the weather had been a lot nicer than in Baku or Tallinn, but was that enough to explain the difference? I didn't have a clue.

All this happened when I was in my late twenties. Later in my career, I often actually enjoyed being alone, which allowed me to create my own daily routine without disturbances. When in 1993 I had my best period ever, I stayed entirely within my own bubble throughout the three important tournaments I played.

In the first, the Zonal Tournament in Brussels, I was so happy in my solitude that I actually became worried when on a free day my wife came to visit me. Although the prospect was pleasant enough in itself, I feared that this would break up my daily routine. Fortunately, my wife, who is also a good chess player and had been through moments like these herself, was aware of the danger and was as careful as I was to minimize any negative impact her visit might have. After she left, I *did* actually lose the very next game (my only loss in the tournament), but then the bubble came back, and by winning my last two games I managed to win the tournament anyway.

The second in the series was the Dutch Championship. This took place in the middle of the turmoil of my wife and I moving house, so the circumstances were not ideal, to say the least. Boredom wasn't the problem here, and neither was loneliness, but the need to close myself off from the outside world was at least as strong as in Brussels. My only hope of playing well under these circumstances was by conserving any small amount of energy I had left for the actual chess. Again, the bubble came to my rescue. Although I was rarely alone physically, mentally I was completely undisturbed and able to fully concentrate on my chess. I actually won the tournament with a round to spare.

Finally, the Biel Interzonal, just a few weeks after the Dutch Championship ended, was the toughest challenge by far. I came to the tournament unprepared, tired from moving house and Elo rating-wise an underdog for qualification for the Candidates Matches. But I also came with the success formula still etched firmly in my mind: stay focused, stay within yourself, let nothing disturb you. Translated in meditation terms this means: concentrate on Now, whatever Now might be. No thoughts about the past, no speculation about the future. I started the tournament shakily enough, but with a little luck I came through the first rounds unscathed, and then the bubble just didn't break anymore. Although the tension increased with every round, I managed to take it all in my stride, and after two gruelling weeks I achieved the biggest success of my career: I qualified for the Candidates Matches.

Based on these and similar experiences, I gradually came to the conclusion that being lonely doesn't necessarily follow from being alone and that being bored wasn't the same as having little to take my mind of chess. It could go either way. The problem was that I found it so very difficult to *control* the situation. It all seemed to depend on pure chance, not on anything I could do.

So, when boredom and loneliness visited me in the meditation hall, I wasn't completely unprepared. Perhaps that is why they didn't knock me out as badly as physical pain had done. To me, they weren't really obstacles — they were old friends from my chess days. I recognized them, acknowledged them ('feeling bored, boredom' or 'feeling lonely, loneliness'), and then they would usually lose their intensity and would often disappear altogether.

Experiencing them like this, in a situation where not only there was nothing else for me to do, but I was under explicit orders to carefully observe whatever would present itself, I finally began to *really* recognize them. Loneliness and boredom are as much a part of the game as everything else. They, too, are characterized by *Dukkha*, *Aniccia* and *Anattā*: Suffering, Impermanence and No-Self. And then I understood why I had never been able to control them. Now that I was in a meditation retreat, where No-Self, no central command to either control or not control, was one of the crucial aspects of what was keeping me busy there, it wasn't even mysterious. The mystery was solved. Yes, loneliness and boredom may appear. But without an 'I' to take ownership of them, they really are perfectly harmless. With no one there, whom could they possibly hurt?

Fear, come and guide me

One very strong emotion that we all know yet don't normally like to acknowledge is fear. It comes in varying degrees of intensity, but whether it is in the shape of a well-founded worry, an unrealistic anxiety, or a wave of sheer panic, fear is almost always present in the back of our mind. From there, it secretly directs our thoughts and our actions.

The conventional take on fear is that it is an unwelcome visitor, and we have to get rid of it as soon as possible. But fear is no more than the emotional colouring of one of the two great driving forces in our minds, the one that instinctively says 'no' to objects perceived.

Its great counterpart, the emotion that equally instinctively says 'yes', and which also comes in different guises and varying degrees of intensity, is of course desire. Where fear pulls us to the left, desire pulls us to the right.

In chess, fear and desire are easily recognizable as the horror of losing and the deep emotional need for success. That doesn't sound so good, but chess players know that these two are indispensable for mobilizing their mental forces in an emergency, which a chess game usually is. You need both the desire to win and the fear of losing to raise your concentration and motivation to the highest possible level.

Whenever I was playing at my very best, fear and desire felt like a pair of bodyguards, guarding and isolating me from the crowd almost against my will. The crowd being the multitude of thoughts that roamed free in my mind and were liable to undermine both my concentration and my motivation. To be shielded like this felt almost painful sometimes, but the result, a complete focus on the present, was a rich reward.

Of this pair of bodyguards, fear was the fear of looking behind me, of seeing my pursuers — my rivals in the tournament — chase me like a pack of wolves. It was a fear that had the effect of a whip — hurting me, driving me mad, but in so doing forcing me to reach heights of concentration that would never have been attainable with my normal crowd of thoughts constantly getting in the way.

On my other side was desire, the desire to get over the finish line, the desperate yearning for the race to be won and to be over. It forced me to look ahead, exclude everything from my vision except the finish line, and experience a desperate urge to cross that line first.

In the meditation hall, desire was always the most visible of the two. The longing for whatever happened to cross my mind (cappuccino, sex, enlightenment) could be very powerful, sometimes making it extremely difficult to keep on 'observing, noting and letting go'. Giving in to these desires often seemed much more urgent than following the instructions.

Fear, on the other hand, used to pop up in the most unexpected ways. In a meditation retreat, there should not normally be anything to fear in the usual sense of the word. Life is much safer there than in the outside world. Still, I noticed that every time I was waiting for my daily interview with the teacher, I found myself becoming increasingly nervous. Even now, I remember vividly the ordeal of sitting on one of those rickety chairs in that long, narrow corridor, awaiting my turn. I would get to the point that I felt my heart racing and sweat breaking out all over my body. Needless to say, this was completely unnecessary, because nothing scary ever happened during these interviews. They were just an opportunity for the meditators to discuss with their teacher any problems or questions they might have in their meditation.

The fact that this innocent encounter could make me so very nervous puzzled me. So I discussed it with several teachers, none of whom came up with a satisfactory answer. At first, I took the rather laconic view that fear, finding its usual outlets blocked, had settled on the run-up to these interviews simply for want of a better opportunity, that it was in a way a random 'choice'. Looking back, though, now that these retreats are a thing of the past, I think it really *was* the fear of human contact that grabbed me by the throat in these moments. After all, these were the only moments during the whole retreat when it was allowed to speak, so they were also the only chance for this particular fear of mine, the fear of having to interact with another human being, to manifest itself.

It is strange that in a world where most people spend so much of their time interacting with other people, this interaction should still be something they fear, but there it is. Nowadays, I am perfectly aware of this particular fear of mine. It still crops up whenever I am about to meet people. But it no longer puzzles or upsets me.

Whenever it comes, it is received by mindfulness. It is felt, it is welcomed, and then it usually loses much of its power, because nothing can deny its own *Aniccia* (Impermanence) and consequently its own *Dukkha* (Suffering) and *Anattā* (No-Self) when seen by mindfulness.

Like desire, fear in itself is not a bad thing. Without it, we would probably not be able to survive as a species. I would certainly not have been able to survive as a high-level chess player. It is just one of those things that feel good sometimes and feel bad at other times. It is nothing to worry about. Fear is nothing to fear.

The real cake

In the previous chapter, I made mention of the daily interviews which were the only occasions when we were allowed to talk during meditation retreats. But it was not the only occasion when we were talked *to*, because on most evenings the teacher would give a lecture, intended to stimulate and motivate the meditators. The subjects of these talks were often partly based on what had been reported to the teacher during the interviews of the day. On one occasion, one of the participants had apparently revealed how much an incident during lunch had disturbed her. She had been the last to come to the counter for dessert, and to her great disappointment had found all the trays empty. Now, in 'real life' you can swear, get angry, demand your dessert even if there isn't any, or walk away. However, in a meditation retreat, all you are supposed to do under any circumstances is to keep following the instructions: 'observe, note and let go'. So that was what she did. But the letting go had clearly not been easy — as it never is in a retreat; an incident like this can haunt you for days — and she had duly reported her feelings of hurt, injustice, desire and disappointment to the teacher during the interview. Now, this experience, the teacher told us, had been a particular stroke of good fortune for her, because it had given her 'the chance to see desire'. 'She got the real cake,' he said. This teaching impressed me enormously at the time, and I made regular use of it when, a few years later, I started doing some teaching myself. But what exactly does it mean?

'She got the real cake.' Unless you want to sound cynical, you can't very well say this to people. You wouldn't normally congratulate them on having had a problematic experience. But when it is a question of making them understand what mindfulness is, it is spot on. No matter what the emotional colouring of an experience may be or how deep the emotion runs, mindfulness means you 'observe, note and let go' at all times, no matter how strong the effects of the emotion are. This is so totally contrary to the way you normally react to unpleasant sensations that your natural instinct will always be to give the emotion free range and let it rip. And because emotions can be so very powerful, it usually requires a little training before people are able to follow the instructions before they are overwhelmed by emotion. I don't know if the woman in question got the message, but I certainly did. When an unpleasant thing happens to you, you can either grieve over the cake that wasn't there or you can see that what you got was *the real cake*.

Did this realization help my chess? I think not. During my first year as a meditator, I once played a game of chess with the express intention of being as mindful as possible. This, I thought, would be an important experiment. Would I play better with a conscious effort at being mindful?

Well, it was a disaster. I forgot my opening theory, missed my opponent's best moves at several vital moments in the game, and ended up losing without a real fight. It was quite an important game too, for it took place in the 1998 Dutch Championship, so it was an expensive lesson. But the conclusion was clear: in chess, concentration is infinitely preferable to mindfulness.

That is to say, if the level of your chess is your priority. There was also a positive side to this experiment, albeit one of a very different kind: I didn't *mind* losing that game. Apparently, mindfulness had resolved the normal emotional pain that comes with a loss. After the game I went home, kissed my wife, ate a hearty dinner, slept well, and the following day I played the next game with renewed vigor (but without mindfulness). And while all this may sound normal to an outsider, every chess player will know that it isn't. Losing hurts.

And it *should* hurt! Playing chess as well as you can isn't something that comes cheap. As soon as you change your priorities, for example from playing chess for real to playing chess for fun, it is only natural to change your mindset. But as long as you are a serious player (and a professional to boot), you just have to give it your best and your best only.

So, in a way the choice is yours: concentration or mindfulness. But perhaps it is fairer to say that some situations require concentration and others require mindfulness. And even that is not fair enough, because in all fairness, there just isn't a choice. The initiative is not with you but with the situation. It is the situation that will draw the quality it requires from you. The thinking comes afterwards — it always does.

The power of concentration

During a meditation retreat, people often discover that focusing their attention on one thing leads to a state of intense concentration that can be very enjoyable indeed. As a result, inexperienced meditators often get stuck in this state of mind, which is also known as 'hyperfocus', 'flow', 'being in the zone', and many other names. And indeed, why should you want to leave paradise when you've just found it?

That is why in *vipassana* meditation this state of intense concentration is considered an obstacle. The temptation to stay where you are and enjoy the sensation causes the one and only instruction for what you came there to do ('observe, note and let go') to be easily forgotten.

Needless to say, there is nothing wrong with this (enjoy yourself!), only it isn't *vipassana*. It may be bliss, but it is not mindfulness.

This was one trap I didn't fall into when I did my first meditation retreats. Being a chess player, this experience was nothing new to me. It stands to reason that being able to concentrate is essential when you play chess, so you just can't help 'getting in the flow' or 'being in the zone' at least every now and then. That is what concentration does for you.

I have had this kind of experience often, and in many different degrees of intensity, but never as powerfully as when, as a relatively inexperienced and nervous twenty-one-year-old, I found myself face to face with the man of the moment, Viktor Korchnoi. Korchnoi had just won the Candidates Tournament and was set to play one of the most epoch-making matches ever later that year, the World Championship Match against Anatoly Karpov.

The year was 1978, and we were playing in the annual Hoogovens Tournament (nowadays the Tata Steel Chess Tournament) in Wijk aan Zee, the Netherlands. Rated far below all the other participants, most of them famous Grandmasters, I was the complete outsider in this field. Not only that, but up to this game I had fully lived up to this role, having lost five and drawn two of my first seven games. Korchnoi, on the other hand, was marching through the tournament as he always did in those days, trampling all opposition, heading for another tournament victory.

Logically speaking, I should have been over-awed, without a chance, without the weaponry to withstand this giant, without hope. But perhaps it was precisely because of all these 'withouts' that I wasn't my normal self that day. The pressure, and therefore the concentration, had become so unbearably great that my normal self had collapsed and disappeared into that black hole known (insofar as it *can* be known) as Now. There were no thoughts, no worries, no expectations, no hopes. There was just fighting spirit, pure fighting spirit, so pure in fact that it lifted me up to a height that I hadn't known existed. Somehow I *became* Korchnoi and absorbed *his* playing level, *his* fighting spirit, *his* stamina. I'm speaking metaphorically, of course, but I can't think of a better image.

Van der Sterren-Korchnoi, Wijk aan Zee 1978

I will skip the usual chess annotations, firstly because I am still flabbergasted whenever I see this game and realize it *was* me playing the white pieces, and secondly because the normal analytical approach seems so pointless when this game was really all about my state of mind.

The game started with a sharp opening variation that was quite popular in those days and on which Korchnoi was a leading expert. The middlegames resulting from this line were almost always unbalanced and therefore very difficult both to judge *and* to play. This game proved no exception, with Korchnoi gaining a pawn and an advantage on the queenside and me building up a slow but strong initiative on the kingside. I felt no fear and just flowed with the battle from move to move, keeping an eye on every nook and cranny of the board, feeling that I was increasing the pressure on his position, but without feeling anything even faintly resembling nerves or uncertainty how to proceed. I didn't think, I *knew* what I had to do — and I did it.

Games were adjourned in those days, and so we adjourned after five hours of play in the middle of what to most people was a difficult and unclear position. To me, however, it was already a fairly clear win. During the two-hour break, I had a light meal together with a friend of mine in a noisy café, and while I would normally say that we discussed the position, in this case it was one-way traffic. I showed him in great detail how the game would continue and he, unbelieving at first but unable to come up with any holes in my variations, could only confirm their correctness. Still, I'm pretty sure he didn't believe for one moment that I was really going to win this game.

Upon resumption, I continued with unbroken concentration. Things went exactly as I had foreseen, and still without nerves, without butterflies, without anything in my mind to distract me from the actual position on the board. When after another two hours of play the game was adjourned for a second time, Korchnoi, having to seal his move, sank into deep thought.

I left the playing hall and showed to a few journalists why the position was winning for me by force, still without excitement, without pride even, still untouchable in my bubble of concentration. Just when I wanted to go to my hotel room (or was it to the bar?), the news reached us that Korchnoi had resigned. Only then did the concentration fade, very slowly at first, a little quicker after a few drinks, and finally completely when I awoke the next day. I was empty then, exhausted, depleted, as if I hadn't played one game against the number two player in the world, but a whole match.

I somehow managed two draws (and one loss)

in the final three rounds and was ill with fatigue for three or four days after the tournament. I actually consulted a doctor, but he couldn't find anything wrong with me. It was purely a matter of stress and the decompression afterwards.

But the one overriding thought in my mind after the game was that I would never ever be able to play this well again in my life, no matter how good a player I would eventually become. I just knew with absolute certainty that this had been the high point of my existence as a chess player, and I also knew that this was both a triumph and a tragedy. For to know at twenty-one years of age that, though your whole life still lies before you, this and only this was the high point, the peak of it all, the one and only once-in-a-lifetime experience — that is both very wonderful and very cruel. Had I known then about *Dukkha*, *Aniccia* and *Anattā*, I would have thoroughly understood them then and there.

1.e4 e6 2.d4 d5 3.♘c3 ♗b4 4.e5 c5 5.a3 ♗xc3+ 6.bxc3 ♘e7 7.♘f3 ♘bc6 8.♗d3 ♕a5 9.0-0 c4 10.♗e2 ♗d7 11.a4 ♘c8 12.♕d2 ♘b6 13.♕g5 ♖g8 14.♖a3 h6 15.♕h5 ♘xa4 16.g3 b5 17.♗d2 ♕d8 18.♖b1 ♕e7 19.♖aa1 a6 20.♘h4 0-0-0 21.♘g2 ♔c7 22.♘e3 ♖a8 23.f4 ♘b6 24.f5 b4 25.♖f1 g6 26.fxg6 ♖xg6

27. ♕f3 ♗e8 28. ♕f4 bxc3 29. ♗xc3 ♕g5
30. ♕f3 a5 31. ♘g2 ♘b4 32. ♘f4 ♖g8 33. ♖fb1
♕d8 34. ♕f1 ♘c6 35. ♖b5 a4 36. ♕b1 ♖a6
37. ♕b2 ♗d7 38. ♕a3 ♘xd4 39. ♕c5+ ♔b7
40. ♗xd4 ♗xb5 41. ♕xb5 a3

42. ♗h5 ♕c7 43. ♘e2 ♕e7 44. ♘c3 ♕d7
45. ♕b4 ♖g5 46. ♖xa3 ♖xa3 47. ♕xb6+ ♔a8
48. ♘b5 ♕b7 49. ♕d8+ ♕b8 50. ♕d7 ♕b7
51. ♕e8+ ♕b8 52. ♕c6+ ♕b7 53. ♕e8+
♕b8 54. ♕c6+ ♕b7 55. ♕d6 ♖axg3+
56. hxg3 ♕xb5 57. ♕f8+ ♔b7 58. ♕xf7+ ♔b8
59. ♔g2 ♕a4 60. ♕f8+ 1-0

Nevertheless, many similar experiences, albeit
on a lower level of intensity, were still to come.
As I mentioned earlier, a chess player just can't
help getting into a state of deep concentration
now and again. Concentration is his job. But in

all the remaining twenty-five years of my career as a competitive chess player, there was perhaps only one occasion where I came marginally close to what happened to me in the above game.

Bareev-Van der Sterren, Biel Interzonal 1993

Position after 19...♗xc8

Earlier, I described how I lived in a bubble of concentration for the whole of this tournament, not worrying or caring about anything. I simply wasn't concerned with either the past or the future. I was just Now and Now only. Amidst an impressive array of world-class players, I was progressing through the event without any of my usual weak moments, maintaining the iron discipline of 'staying in the moment', as it is termed in modern sport psychology. I had withstood the immense pressure successfully for ten out of thirteen rounds, but almost from the moment my game against Bareev started, it turned into a crisis.

My opponent caught me off-guard in my favourite opening, forcing me into a desperate defence, which I thought I had successfully completed when after nineteen moves we reached this position. But then he played

20. ♗f4

and for one short, yet interminably long moment I felt my heart, my position, my bubble, my tournament and the whole world collapse. A deadly cross-pin! Was this then to be the bullet with my name on it, the end of a glorious adventure? And then I saw it:

20...♗c7!

So simple, yet so easy to overlook, especially when calculating in advance. I hadn't been mistaken. Black's position looks awkward, but it will now only take one more move (21...♗d7) and White's attack is halted. The position is equal. My opponent must have felt devastated to the same degree that I felt elated. He kept pushing for a win, made two really bad mistakes, and in the end lost the game, thereby ruining his chances for a qualifying spot into the Candidates Matches. For me, there were still two rounds to go under immense pressure, but with an extra point in my pocket and my bubble fully restored, I managed.

It was one fleeting moment only, but this experience of looking into the abyss and then miraculously discovering that there *was* no abyss is something I will never forget.

To conclude, I would like to point out that this state of deep concentration is not necessarily built on the high pressure of high stakes. The following is probably the most relaxed game I ever played.

Thorstein Thorsteinssson-Van der Sterren, Reykjavik Open 1986

Paradoxically, there is nothing heroic whatsoever about this game: not a famous opponent, nothing much at stake, no beautiful combination. If you play through the moves, you will be surprised to see that there is in fact a complete absence of drama.

1.d4 ♘f6 2.c4 e6 3.♘c3 d5 4.♘f3 ♗e7 5.♗g5 h6 6.♗h4 0-0 7.e3 b6 8.♗e2 ♘bd7 9.cxd5 exd5 10.0-0 ♗b7 11.♕b3 c5 12.♗xf6 ♘xf6 13.dxc5 ♗xc5 14.♖ad1 ♕e7 15.♘b5 ♘e4 16.♘bd4

f5 17.♗b5 ♖ac8 18.♖fe1 g5 19.♖e2 f4 20.exf4
♖xf4 21.g3 ♖f7 22.♔g2 g4 23.♘h4

23...♖xf2+ 24.♖xf2 ♘xf2 25.♘hf5 ♕e4+
26.♔xf2 ♕xf5+ 27.♔g2 ♕e4+ 0-1

And yet I regard this game as one of the highlights of my career, because to play it was an experience of pure bliss. From the first move to the last, I was in that emotionally deeply satisfying state of mind called happiness.

Where this happiness (for want of a better word) came from, so completely unexpectedly, I have no idea. It it true that I had been greatly moved by the beautiful Icelandic countryside with its famous geysers in the morning, but I have often seen beautiful scenery without experiencing an aftereffect of this magnitude.

Fortunately, reasons don't matter. What *is* certain is that I hadn't had a single thought about chess all that morning. When we sat down to play, my mind was empty. I was relaxed, happy to be there, happy to be. It's not important whether this explains why my moves came so effortlessly and were still so powerful as well as precise. It was an exceptional experience that I treasure to this very day.

Can we have quiet, please!

Chess tournaments aren't always run smoothly. The so-called 'open' tournaments, i.e. open to professionals and amateurs alike, can be especially noisy and chaotic. I remember a tournament in Hastings on the English south coast, where the noise in the playing hall was deafening, mainly due to the arbiters who were forever asking for silence at the top of their voices: 'Can we have quiet, please!'

Perhaps the most spectacularly unprofessional event I ever played in was a club match in Leuven, Belgium, where what was a quiet pub at the start of the afternoon gradually transformed into a noisy bar. The rhythm of players finishing their games and starting to talk, shout and drink took over the space. My game was the last one to finish. The turmoil in the room was by then complete, but, having noticed that my opponent's irritation was worse than mine, I was able to relax and let his irritation do the work. Which it did. I won and my opponent went mad.

Whenever my concentration was good, I was fairly immune to things like noise, uncomfortable chairs, bad lighting and other anomalies. But when my concentration was poor, I would often get annoyed by such disturbances. The annoyance would then erode my concentration even more, which would make my annoyance even greater. All too often, the end of the story was that I lost the game first and exploded afterwards.

At least, that is how I saw it when I was still an active player. Nowadays, I am inclined to think that I just didn't feel comfortable on days like that to begin with and managed to successfully project my pre-existing anger, first on my surroundings and then on my chess. It is an awkward truth, but no degree of self-destructiveness is too much for a disgruntled chess player.

In meditation too, anger can be very hard to catch, i.e. to pin down with mindfulness. It's such a strong emotion that it often takes you over before you realize it. Then you just sit there being angry, fantasizing about what you will say or do to people or situations you are angry with, instead of being mindful of the anger ('anger, anger').

This is, of course, exactly the way anger works in daily life as well. It comes in waves, takes you over completely, and then you are just angry, very angry, and you make people suffer for you being angry with them. Again, there is no right or wrong here, but you may find life just a little easier when the waves of anger break on the rocks of mindfulness. Instead of overwhelming you, they might then fizzle out and dissolve into nothingness before any serious damage is done.

In mindfulness, being angry is equivalent to having got one step ahead of yourself. You have missed the anger coming up, and are now immersed in it. You are now angry *with* something or somebody. Had you caught it immediately, there would have been the recognition of the anger only ('anger, anger'). It makes a world of difference.

Here too, the power of mindfulness is, in effect, the Power of Now: *Now* there is anger. It is seen for what it is. It will lose its power. Something else will take its place. It's so easy!

Well, easy in theory, hard in practice, you might object. But a mind that is trained in mindfulness will handle these emotions automatically. You don't have to make an effort. It is in the intensive meditation sessions that an effort must be made. That's where emotions like anger will show their full strength. But if you just stay true to the one and only instruction ('observe, note, and let go'), mindfulness itself will gradually transform into a formidable defensive structure. It will protect you. We are now talking duality, of course, where 'you' are real, or at least 'you' *appear* to be real, but I can't stress it often enough: duality *is* nonduality, only neither of them are aware of it.

In a way, mindfulness works just like modern-day security. You need to show your ID before you are allowed in somewhere. Once you're in, you're fine. Mindfulness works the same way: everything is welcome, but we need to check its ID first. Then life just goes on and we will see what happens next.

In the short period when I was a meditation teacher, I sometimes annoyed 'my' meditators on purpose by giving them a little Dhamma talk *during*, not before or after a sitting. A Dhamma talk is a short talk reminding meditators of the purpose and the finer points of *vipassana* meditation. By thus breaking the silence in the meditation hall, I was aiming not only to keep them awake, but also to provoke some mild anger. Anger doesn't easily come up in the peaceful setting of a meditation retreat, but in real life it is so common that I thought they would do well to try and 'catch' it in a context where they could give it their full and undivided attention.

It was a trick I learned from one of my own teachers, a Thai monk who often arrived up to a full hour late when he came to a retreat to give an evening lecture. It didn't make him popular, but it worked, at least in my case. I got to 'see' an awful lot of anger whenever he did this, but because the circumstances were such that I *had* to be mindful about it, anger gradually lost its 'invisibility cloak' and as a result became much more manageable in real life as well.

I'm not saying that you will be able to eliminate anger from your emotional repertoire. Far from it. That is not what mindfulness does. Anger will always appear whenever it is called for. But mindfulness can be a tool to *handle* your emotions, to prevent them from causing unnecessary damage, both in your mind and in your social life.

The first time I was made aware of this distinction was when I was playing a chess tournament in Antwerp, Belgium, in 1999, where Paul, my friend and first meditation teacher, was also playing. One day I was sitting next to him (not opposite him, we weren't playing against each other), when all of a sudden I heard him banging his fist on the table and muttering some prime Dutch curses under his breath. What had happened? He had made a bad mistake and was now suddenly losing a game that he had thought he was on the verge of winning. I was astonished by this outburst, a severe break of tournament etiquette, especially coming from him, a long-time meditator and my own meditation teacher to boot. If even he was still capable of an outburst like that after twenty years of intensive meditation, what was the good of meditating at all?

But when he invited me for a drink after our games were finished, I slowly began to understand. He was now perfectly calm again and even looked happy. Anger had come, it had had its moment of 'glory', and then it had disappeared, not leaving any traces of resentment or shame. Mindfulness had made the anger leave his system quietly after it had had its say. Other chess players would have lamented the mistake they had made (or the outburst of anger) for hours or even days, unable to let it go. It could have affected their next game as well and could quite possibly have ruined their entire tournament. That's what making a bad mistake can do to a chess player!

But Paul had not lost more than what had become unavoidable: just the one game. Not his humour, not his tournament. The next day he just continued as if nothing had happened and played a great game.

Chess is my life

Several of the most famous chess players in recent history have called their autobiographies *Chess Is My Life* or a variation thereof. This is definitely not a coincidence, and I suspect that in fact *every* chess player who writes a book about themselves would like to use that title, not just the famous ones. When chess really grabs you, it may very well take over your life. But what is life?

I concluded one of the previous chapters by saying, 'The initiative lies not with you, but with the situation.' I would now like to go one step further and replace 'the situation' with 'life'. Once you realize that the initiative never lies with 'you' because the whole concept of 'you and me' is shaky, the question arises: what then? If it isn't *my* life, then whose is it? This is one of the unanswerable questions, because it points *beyond* the limits of human thinking. And while human thinking is undeniably very good at creating a certain order and logic *within* its own sphere, it cannot go where it cannot go.

When this is clearly seen, it also becomes clear that whatever we may think, say or write, is by definition only a translation. It's a translation of what cannot be translated, which is the unthinkable, unspeakable and incomprehensible that lies outside the scope of human expression. And no matter how good or bad a translation may be, it is always just that, only a translation.

This frees the way for another realization, namely that an answer to unanswerable questions *can* be given, if — and only if — it is understood what an answer really is: a translation of the untranslatable. No matter how good or how bad an answer is, it's never, *never* more than a translation. It shouldn't be mistaken for 'the real thing'. A translation is a pointer put into words.

Now, the perfect instrument for turning a mere statement into a pointer is the paradox. A mere statement of fact remains by necessity within the sphere of human thinking. But a paradox makes a statement while at the same time refuting that statement. Thus, the mind, while unable to go beyond its limitations, is made aware *of* its limitations. This will cause it to look back and reflect on what it has just stated, but now from the perspective of being at the limit of what is humanly possible.

So, when I say 'the initiative never lies with you, it lies with life', this should not be taken as a plain statement of fact, even an incorrect one. For how can I say this when to the human mind it is so blatantly clear that it is not true, that on the contrary I am very much the person who takes the initiative?

It's a paradox. What I try to 'translate' in this way is that there *is* only life. But since the human mind can only see a series of apparent individuals who together make up the whole of its experience, terms like 'you' and 'me' are its only mode of expression. When the mind is made to look at itself (and others) from the perspective of being on that borderline between 'here' and 'beyond', it might just see that 'you' and 'me' are merely a reflection of what cannot be seen, in the mirror of what *can* be seen.

From that viewpoint, the title *Chess is my life* may be interpreted as *Life, living itself by being me, a chess devotee*. This is precisely how I see my chess career now, after having been 'brainwashed' by many years of meditation. I use the term brainwashing here in its literal sense, which is simply to clean your brain and restore it to its original state, a state where it recognizes that words such as 'I', 'you', 'me' and 'mine' are just tools of communication. You learn to use them as such when you are very young, then forget they were ever something like acquired knowledge.

In a way, meditation is an attempt to go back to those early years before you learned to use 'I' and 'you'. When practicing the method of 'observing, noting, and letting go', you simply don't need these communication tools. If this practice is sustained over a period of hours or even days on end, it is no more than natural that at some point these tools are seen for what they really are.

When I was a student, I lived with an elderly couple who weren't very interested in chess. They used to call it my 'hobby of pushing around wooden *"poppetjes"*,' the Dutch word for dolls and figurines. This is exactly right. Playing chess *is* pushing figurines around. But once you become a serious chess player, you totally forget that this is in fact what you are doing, because you can no longer look at it from the outside.

I should add, though, that this is not a matter of right or wrong. From the outside point of view, playing chess is indeed pushing *'poppetjes'* around. But seen from inside — and once you get inside there is no turning back — playing chess means entering a different world, where life is dictated by the laws of chess and where pushing *'poppetjes'* around translates as playing moves.

So what *I* meant and what *they* meant was exactly the same. We were just speaking different languages.

In a nutshell, this is what nonduality is all about. Seeing that opposites are opposites only in the mirror of the visible, i.e. the outside world, not when looked at from within. The dualistic or outside view of the slogan *Chess is my life* is that this is the story of a person devoting his life to chess. The nondualistic or inside view is that there *is* only Life, going about its business. And that business appears to be a person who devotes his life to chess.

And there is another similarity between chess and life. Both are based on the principle 'play by the rules'. In chess, this is clear: you play by the rules of chess. But in life it is exactly the same: the rules of society dictate that you accept the existence of an 'I', a 'you', etc., as reality, or you can't play. Play by the rules. That's what we are all doing.

The Endgame

Facing the double-edged sword

Within a few years of reaching my career high by qualifying for the Candidates Matches of 1994, I began to feel that something was wrong. My results were getting worse, my motivation was waning and, worst of all, even my interest in chess seemed to be deteriorating. This was an entirely new situation for me. Chess had always given me an interest and a direction in life. It had been the automatic steering mechanism in my mind that kept me going, always onward. But now there didn't seem to be an onward anymore. Could it be that I was going backward instead? And if so, what would that involve?

It was an idea that didn't appeal to me. I tried all I could think of to get my motivation and my interest back. I changed my opening repertoire, bought a new computer, started a diary, tried to be more relaxed. But nothing worked. On the contrary, that sinking feeling of having reached the end of the road gradually became stronger and stronger. But what could I do? A life without chess seemed totally insecure, both financially and psychologically. Chess had always been my life, what else was there for me?

But parallel to this negative development, I was also beginning to feel the positive effects of my growing interest in philosophy. As a human being, I was beginning to feel more mature, more at ease with the world and, yes, perhaps even more willing to accept the decline of my chess powers. But this kind of acceptance is a double-edged sword, and I knew it. The human being may gain by it, but the chess player loses.

So, even though by now meditation had shown me how futile emotions like worrying were, I was deeply worried.

The reality, of course, was that the chess player had by then long lost, though he didn't know it, long before the double-edged sword of accepting the inevitable had come into focus. Neither did the human being know that he had already won. It goes to show how unimportant knowing is. Knowing, like thinking, always comes afterwards only, when it is a matter of looking back and reflecting on what has happened. Knowledge is just a story. It's the story made of happenings after they have occurred.

And what occurred was that I ended my career as an active professional chess player in 2001, when I was forty-five years old. I did this out of a growing awareness of the inevitable decline that every chess player has to face sooner or later, but also because I had reached a point where the fearful prospect of jumping into the unknown had mellowed into an acceptable risk. I had no idea where I was going, but I trusted life to have something in store for me yet. Whatever the future would hold, I — more or less — trusted it to be right for me.

This too is only a story, a rational explanation of what happened long after it happened, but my theory is that it was mindfulness that made this jump into the unknown possible. After three years of meditation, including a series of intensive ten-day retreats, fear of the unknown had lost its hold over me. It was still there, but had lost the strength to pin me down in a place where I didn't want to be anymore. The strict discipline of observing, noting and letting go had relaxed the old straitjacket. I was free to go, so I went.

Is that a happy ending? Again, this is just storytelling, but I'm inclined to say yes. I had come to a point where the energy of being a serious and ambitious chess player had exhausted itself in many years of intense competition. Whether this was because of my advancing years, my inability to adapt to the multitude of changes that were then taking place in the chess world, or because of some other reason, is unimportant. It happened, that's all there is to say about it. Like a marriage ending in divorce, there is no good or bad about it. These things happen. It is the fundamental reality of *Aniccia* or Impermanence, which cannot help but saddle the individual with some measure of *Dukkha* or Suffering. But the saving grace is always that there *is* no individual: *Anattā*.

Mindfulness helped me to realize and to accept that the end of my chess career had come. It also helped me to make the break without the mental pain that might so easily have accompanied it. Taking away the *idée fixe* that everything always happens to *me*, mindfulness opened up the mental space to just let things happen the way they happen, including the fear and the insecurity that might (and did) occur whenever there is change. It's not the change that hurts you, it is the idea that there is a you that can be hurt.

The gateway to the unknown

Leeuwarden, June 2001, the Dutch Championship. This, my last tournament, was a painful one. To begin with, in the eyes of the world I suffered the ignominy of coming last. Even worse was the emptiness that I felt throughout the tournament: the feeling of no longer belonging there, of having outlived my chess life. But worst of all was the shocking realization that I just didn't care anymore, neither about my results nor about the level of my play. The chess player in me was dead.

But having passed through the gate, I was immediately aware of a feeling of relief. I was in unknown territory, didn't have a clue what was in store for me, but it felt right to be there. It felt like freedom. Freedom, of course, is a meaningful word in duality only. In nonduality it is as meaningless as every other word, for without an 'I' to be either free or unfree, what are we talking about? So, let's talk duality.

The first thing I did in this new freedom was to deepen my involvement with my meditation centre in Amsterdam. I had been doing volunteer work there practically from the time I started to meditate, but at the invitation and under the supervision of the very same teacher who had helped me survive my first ten-day retreat, I now took up the role of teacher myself. I was proud of this 'promotion', which opened up new vistas in my life. Could being a meditation teacher be my new identity?

For a few years, everything seemed to point that way. I enjoyed my new role. My responsibilities and activities in the meditation centre gradually widened. Being both a student and a teacher of meditation not only deepened my insight into meditation itself, it also opened my eyes to what we were actually teaching.

Yet, gradually, in conversations and meetings with my fellow teachers and meditators, I began to feel that we were taking too much 'theory' for literal truth. Too much duality for nonduality. While I respected the teachings and traditions of the Southeast-Asian countries where our particular brand of meditation technique originates (Thailand and Myanmar), I instinctively felt that one element at least of the traditional teachings was dealt with too rationally and therefore too one-sidedly. This was the axiom that 'we', the teachers, should methodically guide our students to enlightenment. If there was one thing I had found out, it was that there *are* no stages to enlightenment. Worse, there is no enlightenment — except that *everything* is enlightenment.

I'm fully aware that this is moving away from logic and taking refuge in a paradox. But it is my firm conviction that talking about that which cannot be talked about can only be done in paradoxes. Any attempt to be rational or methodical will always fail utterly in the end.

Ultimately, this isn't about right or wrong. But I feel that I would betray the insight I have gained if I didn't emphasize that it's not knowing, but not-knowing that really matters. Enlightenment is something that can perhaps be touched upon in poetry and paradoxes, but not in rational thinking. And mapping out a route to enlightenment is just fooling people (and yourself).

So there I was, a teacher with nothing to teach. But I soon discovered that precisely this 'teaching nothing' was something I greatly enjoyed. I began to write articles and books about the zillions of ways in which duality and nonduality are engaged in a continual dance on the altar of truth. It's what I still love most: finding words for what can't be formulated. Doing what can't be done. Failing and succeeding at the same time. Seeing this neither as failure nor as success, but in a wholly different new way: a non-competitive way, a nondualistic way. Dare I call it ... Love?

The Afterlife

In the silence that followed my meditation career, chess unexpectedly resurfaced. But this time it came without the competitiveness that had been such an integral part of it in my professional years. By now in my mid-fifties, I couldn't reasonably expect to regain my former playing strength, and I never tried to. I still play the occasional game nowadays, but never in a competitive, always in a social context.

What is left is the pure love of chess. The appreciation of its beauty, its myriad possibilities, always new, always different, yet always within the same inviolable framework that I knew so well. Instead of the competition, the immense pleasure I take in being a spectator, a fan, a commentator and a writer about chess has become my motivation. Nothing makes me happier now than to follow the games of the elite players online or to talk or write about chess. I have finally become a real amateur (a word I used to despise), i.e. someone who truly loves chess, not for its prospects of personal glory, but for its beauty. The joy is no longer in the games *I* play, but in the games I watch *others* play.

To use the gladiator metaphor one last time, I am now like a gladiator who after his death finds himself in gladiator heaven, which turns out to be the very same arena were he has spent his entire life, but with the crucial difference that he is now in the stands, watching others fight instead of doing the fighting himself.

And what about mindfulness? Surprisingly perhaps, I could almost repeat verbatim about mindfulness that which I just said about chess. I don't practice formal meditation anymore, but mindfulness has become a fundamental part of my everyday mindset. I'm not normally aware of it, but I'm absolutely certain that, invisibly, unknowably, unstoppably, it continues to guide not *me* but life itself through 'my' life and beyond.

In life, like in chess, I have become an amateur, driven not by competition, but by love. It is the pure love of the game that I am talking about. Whether that game is called chess or life is immaterial. In the end, there *is* only one game, and love is its playing field.

Does that sound nonsensical? Good! No statement can possibly be true unless it is untrue in equal measure. That is the joy and also the secret of playing with words. And perhaps, perhaps, it's also the secret of life.

Epilogue

If this book has inspired you to take up meditation yourself or to try and inject some mindfulness into your chess, I must warn you that meditation is not something to be taken lightly. Interfering with your 'normal' state of mind (even if it isn't a particularly pleasant one) can have all sorts of unwanted results, especially if you are a vulnerable person.

First, I would never recommend starting by yourself, without any guidance. Videos can be useful, but I would recommend that you join a group with a competent teacher, before you take the plunge of doing solitary meditation at home.

Second, every chess player develops a certain ritual over the years, a set of things to do or not to do that helps them build up their concentration before a game. If you are wondering whether meditation would be a valuable addition to *your* particular routine, I can only tell you that, of course, meditation *could* be a useful inclusion, but this is personal. I myself practiced meditation every day in my final years as a chess player, so it was only natural for me to stick to this routine on days when I was playing chess. If you're not a regular meditator already, I wouldn't particularly recommend trying it before a game. But if you are, I'm sure you don't need my advice. Advice is a very dangerous thing to give anyway. I advise you never to take any, not even mine.

Recommended further reading

There are very many different translations of the *Bhagavad Gita* in many different languages. The book I bought in New York was a Penguin Classic, translated into English from the Sanskrit original by Juan Mascaró. It splendidly conveys the poetic nature of the original. I found it both illuminating and highly inspiring.

Of the *Tao Te Ching*, there are perhaps even more translations, which is understandable once it is realized how little is known about the work and how uncertain the original text really is. It wouldn't surprise me if every serious reader of this classic ended up making his own translation. That's what the book did to me.

The list of works on Buddhism is endless. I am

by no means an authority on the subject, but I found the following works both inspiring and informative:

— Walpola Rahula: *What the Buddha Taught*
— John Stevens: *Three Zen Masters*
— Stephen Batchelor: *Verses from the Center*

The Open Secret was Tony Parsons' first attempt to describe the indescribable. His later writings are based on the many meetings and talks he has since given all over the world, in particular on the many questions that people have asked him. Reading the first of these that fell into my hands, *All There Is*, instantly robbed me of all my illusions and left me with an empty, but clear head. *Nothing Being Everything* and *This Freedom* are equally powerful.

And if that's not enough nonduality reading for you, there are always the collected sayings and talks of the great twentieth century Indian sages, Ramana Maharshi and Nisargadatta Maharaj. The latter's recommendation to just sit 'with nothing but "I am" in your mind', though not *vipassana*, is, if anything, an even more powerful meditation technique. But that's another story...

Acknowledgments

This book would not have been written without Remmelt Otten, publisher of New in Chess. He suggested it, convinced me that it could be done and was always ready with inspiring comments when I needed them most.

I am also greatly indebted to David Riordan for his careful reading of my manuscript and his wonderful critique. His was a crucial help in making this a better book.

Finally, I would like to thank my wife, Hanneke, without whose constant encouragement none of my books would ever have materialized, least of all this one.

Published by New In Chess, Alkmaar,
The Netherlands
www.newinchess.com

Cover Design: Mara Evers
Editor: David L. Riordan, Marigold Editorial
Typography: Sander Pinkse
Proofreading: Peter Boel
Production: Anton Schermer

Have you found any errors in this book?
Please send your remarks to editors@newinchess.
com. We will collect all relevant corrections on the
Errata page of our website www.newinchess.com and
implement them in a possible next edition.

ISBN 978-90-833-3652-7 (hardcover)
ISBN 978-90-833-4791-2 (paperback)